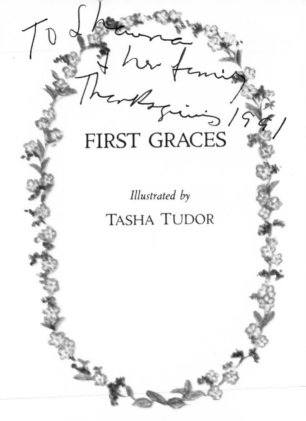

To Shawna
& her family
Thanksgiving 1991

FIRST GRACES

Illustrated by

TASHA TUDOR

Random House New York

Library of Congress Cataloging-in-Publication Data:
Tudor, Tasha. First graces. SUMMARY: Twenty-one short
graces include several for meals and ones for the New Year,
Easter, springtime, school, the Fourth of July, United
Nations Day, Thanksgiving, and Christmas.
1. Children—Prayer books and devotions—English. [1. Prayer
books and devotions.   2. Grace at meals] I. Tudor, Tasha,
ill.   BV265.F54   1989   242'.82   88-306731
ISBN: 0-394-84409-2

Manufactured in the United States of America
1 2 3 4 5 6 7 8 9 0

To

POLLY THAYER STARR

WITH LOVE AND

GRATITUDE

Dear Lord, I offer thee this day
All I shall think, or do, or say.

For food, and all thy gifts of love,
  We give thee thanks and praise.
Look down, O Father, from above
  And bless us all our days.

For what we are about to receive,
the Lord make us truly thankful.

Some hae meat, and canna eat,
    And some wad eat that want it;
But we hae meat and we can eat,
    And sae the Lord be thankit.
                    Robert Burns

10

For every cup and plateful,
God make us truly grateful.
A. S. T. Fisher

Bless, O Lord, this food to our use,

And us to thy loving service.

God, we thank you for this food,
For rest and home and all things good;
For wind and rain and sun above,
But most of all for those we love.

Maryleona Frost

Be present at our table, Lord;
Be here and everywhere adored.
Thy creatures bless, and grant that we
May feast in paradise with thee.
John Wesley

We thank thee, Lord, for happy hearts,
For rain and sunny weather.
We thank thee, Lord, for this our food,
And that we are together.

Emilie Fendall Johnson

Jesus, friend of little children,
Be a friend to me;
Take my hand and ever keep me
Close to thee.

Walter J. Mathans

The Lord my pasture shall prepare,
And feed me with a shepherd's care;
His presence shall my wants supply,
And guard me with a watchful eye.

Joseph Addison

24

At the New Year

Thanks be to thee, Lord Jesus,
For another year to serve thee,
To love thee,
And to praise thee.

A Birthday Grace

God made the sun
  And God made the tree,
God made the mountains
  And God made me.

I thank you, O God,
For the sun and the tree,
For making the mountains
And for making me.

Leah Gale

29

On Easter

Joyfully, this Easter day,
I kneel, a little child, to pray;
Jesus, who hath conquered death,
Teach me, with my every breath,
To praise and worship thee.

Sharon Banigan

SPRINGTIME

All things bright and beautiful,
All creatures great and small,
All things wise and wonderful,
The Lord God made them all.

Each little flower that opens,
Each little bird that sings,
He made their glowing colors,
He made their tiny wings.
Mrs. C. F. Alexander

FOR SCHOOL

At home or at school
Wherever I may go
One thought I remember
That is good to know.
It stays in my heart
A happy little song
That God takes care of me
The whole day long.

J. Lilian Vandevere

On the Fourth of July

Our fathers' God, to thee,
Author of liberty,
 To thee we sing:
Long may our land be bright
With freedom's holy light;

Protect us by thy might,
Great God, our King.
Samuel F. Smith

United Nations Day

North, South, East, and West,
May thy holy name be blessed:
Everywhere around the sun,
May thy holy will be done.

FOR THANKSGIVING

May God give us grateful hearts
And keep us mindful
Of the need of others.

CHRISTMAS EVE

What can I give Him,
    Poor as I am?
    If I were a shepherd,
I would bring Him a lamb;
    If I were a wise man,
    I would do my part;
But what can I give Him?
    Give Him my heart.
                Christina Rossetti

CHRISTMAS DAY

Glory to God in the highest,
and on earth peace,
good will toward men.

Luke 2:14

T. Tudor

WE OFFER sincere thanks to the various publishers and copyright holders for permission to reprint: "Dear Lord, I offer thee this day" from *Prayers for All Occasions*, Forward Movement Publications of the Episcopal Church; "For food, and all thy gifts of love" from *A Little Book of Prayers and Graces*, by Quail Hawkins, illustrated by Marguerite de Angeli, copyright 1941, 1952 by Doubleday & Co., Inc.; "For every cup and plateful" from *An Anthology of Prayers*, by A. S. T. Fisher, copyright 1934 by Longmans, Green & Co.; "God, we thank you for this food," by Maryleona Frost, *Wee Wisdom*; "We thank thee, Lord, for happy hearts" from *A Little Book of Prayers*, by Emilie Fen-